Entrepreneur

Elon Musk:
7 Keys to Business Success

By: Dave O'Brian

© **Copyright 2016 by Oakmont Fox - All rights reserved.**

The follow eBook is reproduced below with the goal of providing information that is as accurate and reliable as possible. Regardless, purchasing this eBook can be seen as consent to the fact that both the publisher and the author of this book are in no way experts on the topics discussed within and that any recommendations or suggestions that are made herein are for entertainment purposes only. Professionals should be consulted as needed prior to undertaking any of the action endorsed herein.

This declaration is deemed fair and valid by both the American Bar Association and the Committee of Publishers Association and is legally binding throughout the United States.

Furthermore, the transmission, duplication or reproduction of any of the following work including specific information will be considered an illegal act irrespective of if it is done electronically or in print. This extends to creating a secondary or tertiary copy of the work or a recorded copy and is only allowed with express written consent from the Publisher. All additional right reserved.

The information in the following pages is broadly considered to be a truthful and accurate account of facts and as such any inattention, use or misuse of the information in question by the reader will render any resulting actions solely under their purview. There are no scenarios in which the publisher or the original author of this work can be in any fashion deemed liable for any hardship or damages that may befall them after undertaking information described herein.

Additionally, the information in the following pages is intended only for informational purposes and should thus be thought of as universal. As befitting its nature, it is presented without assurance regarding its prolonged validity or interim quality. Trademarks that are mentioned are done without written consent and can in no way be considered an endorsement from the trademark holder.

Table of Contents

INTRODUCTION 1

Chapter 1: Who Is Elon Musk? 2

Chapter 2: 7 Keys To Business Success 9

Chapter 3: 6 Simple Exercises To Get You Started 33

Conclusion 50

INTRODUCTION

There are few people who can claim to have achieved the kind of success that seems to come so easily to Elon Musk, the founder of Tesla Motors and SpaceX. His drive and seemingly-limitless ambition have had a lasting impact on technology, science, and the direction of progress.

So how does he do it? Does Elon Musk have some kind of superpower? Does he know something you don't? Is it possible for someone like you to make the kind of waves in history that this South African-born entrepreneur did?

Actually, yes. There is no special potion to conjure, no magic spell to recite, no rare crystal one must attain to follow in Musk's footsteps. All it really takes is determination, dedication to a goal, and recognizing and accepting personal limitations.

This book is designed to show you how, by implementing a few easy-to-understand philosophies and strategies, you can put yourself on the path to success that led Elon Musk—and many others before him—to achieve great things never before thought possible. It's not just thinking outside the box. It's thinking outside yourself. It's about thinking about more than money.

Don't believe it? Just read on and find out for yourself.

Chapter 1: Who Is Elon Musk?

Elon Musk was born in 1971, in Transvaal, South Africa. The oldest child of a dietician and an electromechanical engineer, Musk was introduced at a very young age to the dual realities of entrepreneurship and technological advancements. His parents divorced two years after he was born, and Musk spent most of his remaining childhood with his father, the electromechanical engineer. (His mother moved back to Canada, where she was from.)

It's not surprising, then, that by the time he was ten years old Musk was already teaching himself all kinds of things about computer programming. At the age of twelve, he sold the code for a simple program he had written—a video game called Blastar—to a PC magazine for five hundred dollars. (That's almost a thousand dollars in today's money. Still not a huge amount of money to you and I, perhaps, but imagine having that in your bank account when you were in the seventh grade!)

It was his first taste of success, but only the tip of the iceberg. But he also learned that success comes at a price. Despite his genius, or perhaps, in fact, because of it, Musk was often subjected to severe bullying at school. Believe it or not, he even ended up in the hospital once when a group of boys threw him down a flight of stairs, and then beat him so severely that he lost consciousness. This sort of extreme adversity may have hobbled the dreams of other children, but for Elon Musk it must have only made his ambitions that much stronger. Unfortunately it wouldn't be the last time he faced such bullying, even well into his adulthood.

Elon Musk graduated from high school in 1989, and moved to Canada just after his eighteenth birthday, already a citizen there at this point thanks to his Canadian-born mother. (He's now a U.S. Citizen, but that wouldn't happen for more than a decade, in 2002.) After attending college in Ontario for undergraduate studies, he transferred to the University of Pennsylvania where, in 1992, he earned dual bachelors degrees in Physics and Economics. (Again, all signs point to the Elon Musk who would, two decades later, change the world by introducing the first affordable and best-selling electric car named after one of his own personal idols, Nikola Tesla.) In 1995, he began pursuing a PhD at Stanford University but he ended up leaving the program without completing it; his business aspirations were too great, and he couldn't wait to get started.

Since that time, he has founded or been involved in the development of numerous companies and projects, some with more runaway success than others. His first company, Zip2, which he founded with his brother Kimbal in 1995, was a web software company that had contracts with several American newspapers to provide online city guides. Despite being the company's co-founder, Musk was denied the chance to become CEO by the company's board of directors, but he later earned $22M from the sale of Zip2 to computer industry giant Compaq.

A few years later, Musk co-founded a financial services and email payment company called X.com, which eventually merged with what would become global online payment juggernaut PayPal. Although Musk was the CEO of the company for a time, he was demoted from that position in 2000 over disputes with the board members regarding his plans for the future of the company. (He reportedly wanted to use Windows for the software's infrastructure, as opposed to the Unix-based system it had been using all along.) He received $165M from the sale of PayPal in 2002, when it was bought by eBay.

Shortly after that, Musk founded the company SpaceX (short for Space Exploration Technologies) with the intent of creating a "true spacefaring civilization." But the road to that company's creation was some of the most challenging and life-changing road he had traveled to that point. Musk had made several trips to Russian rocket factories, taking along different people he knew who were experts in the field of aerospace and orbital sciences. His intention was to discuss the possibility of purchasing intercontinental ballistic missiles (ICBMs), because he had figured out that the rockets could be used to develop a way to send a payload to Mars—namely, an experimental greenhouse that would grow crops for food. It was his way of trying to rekindle the publics' waning interest in space exploration. Musk has always had a fascination with space travel, and it's his belief that, given the climate crisis facing humanity on Earth, expanding our civilization to the stars is the only way we will avoid a mass extinction event.

To say that Musk's visits to the Russian factory were met with disdain would be an understatement. During one visit he was actually spat on by one of the chief Russian designers who felt Musk was too young and unqualified to be there. Of course, given his experiences as a child, Musk was no stranger to bullying, and his determination was unhampered. He just decided he wouldn't be buying any ICBMs from the Russians after all. In fact, he determined that the cost would be far less for him to simply found his own company and build the rockets himself, so that's exactly what he did. Using $100M of the money he had earned up to that point, he founded SpaceX in 2002. And this time, he was finally going to stay in the role of CEO.

Since its founding, SpaceX has brought many "firsts" into the world: The first privately-funded liquid-fueled vehicle to put a satellite into orbit. The first private vehicle to rendezvous with the International Space Station. The first orbital rocket to land on the same spot where it was launched (a vital step in making the future of private space flight affordable). The company is the largest private manufacturer of rocket engines, and those engines also hold the record for highest thrust-to-weight ratio. SpaceX isn't obliterating the competition because, for all intents and purposes, there doesn't seem to be any competition.

And then of course there's perhaps his most famous endeavor, Tesla Motors. It's the company which arguably made Elon Musk a household name, but he didn't even start it himself. It was founded by two other men, Martin Eberhard and Marc Tarpenning, in 2003. Musk came onboard around 2004, taking the lead to acquire investors for the company. Although Tarpenning was initially Tesla's CEO, he was asked to resign by the board of directors in 2007, and in 2008—after the financial crisis that hobbled much of American industry—Elon Musk took over as CEO and product architect. He continues to hold both titles within the company in 2016.

Musk's philosophy in plotting out the success of Tesla Motors was nothing short of insightful. He oversaw the development of the Roadster, a two-seat electric sports car that would have a limited production run and sell for a high price to those auto and electric enthusiasts that could afford it. The car debuted in 2008 and only 2,500 of them were made. But Musk's goal was never to cater to the rich and powerful, he simply saw the Roadster as the company's meal ticket, a way to afford to produce the cars that he felt would really have an impact on the world's environmental crisis. Using the profits from the limited but lucrative sales of the Roadster, Musk developed and produced the Model S. Unlike the impractical Roadster, the Model S was a luxury sedan that was markedly more affordable—although still out of reach to the majority of Americans. Tesla launched the Model S in 2012, producing fifteen to twenty cars per week. By 2015, that number had grown to more than a thousand a week.

And yet it still wasn't the endgame for Elon Musk. Like the Roadster before it, to Musk, the Model S was simply a means to an end. The incredibly popular vehicle increased profits for the company enough to allow Tesla to develop more vehicles with even wider appeal. In late 2015, the company launched the SUV counterpart to the Model S, the Model X. And 2017 is the target year for the launch of the Tesla's ultimate dream car, the Model 3. Predicted to sell for less than $30k each, the Model 3 is the affordable family electric car that Musk has been working toward. And he used all of his previous successes to help fund it.

There's also SolarCity, the company Musk founded in 2006, reported after he attended Burning Man Festival, to try to bring solar energy into the mainstream. As of 2016, SolarCity is the second largest solar provider in the United States, and is working with his other company, Tesla Motors, to use electric vehicle motors to enhance the effectiveness of rooftop solar panels. And OpenAI, the non-profit research center Musk founded in 2015 to study the development of safe and beneficial artificial intelligence.

What's next on the horizon? Only Elon Musk knows for sure. For one thing, there's the Hyperloop, his proposal for a large-scale transportation system based on pneumatic tubes. Musk envisions a future where goods and people are shipped at airplane speeds across the country—and even around the world—in simple tubes, traveling just above the ground, floating on magnetic rails. It may seem far-fetched, but so did the idea of the Model S at one point. So did the SpaceX "Dragon," the vehicle that rendezvoused with the International Space Station.

Then there's his philanthropic endeavors, the stuff he does simply for the sake of doing good. He regularly donates millions of dollars to worthy causes, including a $10M donation to the Future of Life Institute, to further research benign and beneficial artificial intelligence.

Although seemingly anything is possible with the various companies and projects Musk is responsible for, one thing seems clear from his track record: he is never satisfied to stop, always compounding his cumulative successes into greater and greater success. And what does he consider success? Clearly it's not simply financial gain, not for its own sake anyway. He has stated from time to time that the goal with his various endeavors is no less than the advancement of human evolution and the preservation of the global consciousness. Musk wants to send humans to Mars, and beyond. He wants us to not only survive, but to thrive.

Does that sound like a typical CEO to you? Does that sound like the quintessential Type-A, financially-savvy business insider? Probably not. And yet Elon Musk is, without reasonable argument, one of the most successful and important businesspeople of the 21st century. Is he an outlier? An anomaly whose success is merely circumstantial? That would be hard to believe. Perhaps, instead, Musk's success is directly attributable to his personal philosophies, motivations, and expectations. Perhaps if someone else—you, for instance—were to mimic those qualities, that person could be as successful in their own life as Elon Musk has been in his.

Chapter 2: 7 Keys To Business Success

There are lots of paths to success, as many paths as there are people to walk them. But a person like Elon Musk walks a slightly different path than most would expect for someone so wildly successful in business. His path is less about financial strategies and emerging markets, and more about personal philosophies and forward thinking.

1: Trust Yourself

It may be counterintuitive to start this book with this piece of advice, but: don't listen to what everyone else tells you to do. There have been hundreds of hugely successful businesspeople over the years, and I can promise you that not one of them got to where they are merely by following someone else's advice. Not merely, mind you. Obviously good businesspeople get where they are by surrounding themselves with smart people—usually people smarter than they are, in fact— who give them good, solid advice. That's not what I'm talking about, of course. But you have to guess that not one of those CEOs or business magnates or captains of industry got their start simply by picking up a book one day that told them how to be successful, nor did they just attend some seminar where an overpaid "expert" told them which business they needed to be in. That's a nice rags-to-riches fairytale, but the fact is that the kind of people who would expect that method to work are not, I'm sorry to say, the kind of people who end up changing the world.

Think about it. Can you imagine Andrew Carnegie, J.P. Morgan, Warren Buffet or Walt Disney sitting there, wide-eyed, listening to that seminar? An empty vessel just waiting to be filled with information on what to do, where to go, how to invest? I certainly can't. Each of those people started by seeing a need that was going unfulfilled, and placing themselves in just the right position to fill that need. They weren't sitting on the couch, watching TV and waiting for just the right self-help book or infomercial or "make money working from home" scheme to fall into their laps. Congratulate yourself for reading this book, but know that you have to apply the principles contained to your own life if you want to truly make a difference and become successful.

I'm not saying you shouldn't take advice, but I am saying you should trust your own gut. Nobody knows you better than you do. Nobody knows what you are capable of, what you are interested in, what you are passionate about, better than the person you see in the mirror every night before you go to bed and every morning when you wake up. Read all the books you care to, take all the seminars you can stand, but ultimately listen only to yourself. You will make mistakes, yes, and you will fail. But you will do so knowing you have no one to blame except for yourself, and that will be a kind of comfort in the end. Because when you rise again from the ashes of each failure—as you must—you will also know that you alone are the reason you can do that. You are self-sufficient, you are strong, you are going to change the world. Other people may tell you you're great, and that you're going to change the world—or they may tell you you're the worst, that you are incapable of changing the world, and that you're wasting your time on whatever it is you're doing. Who is right and who is wrong? Ultimately, that's up to you to decide. Just because someone tells you you're short doesn't mean you are. If someone told you you have blonde hair but you know you have brown hair, you would obviously know they're either crazy or they're trying to mess with you, right? Either way, you wouldn't suddenly start to doubt the color of your hair. So why should you listen when they tell you don't know what you're doing? Don't you know your own mind better than they do?

But you have to accept to other side of that same coin: don't let it go to your head when people call you a genius or tell you you have everything figured out. Maybe you are a genius, and maybe you do have everything figured out, but again that's only something you know. If you feel confident, be confident, but don't let others confidence in your give you a false sense of security. Many people have failed because they let those around them build up their egos to the point where they stopped questioning their own motivations, or even paying attention to them. They simply coasted on whatever nice words they were hearing, and figured all their adoring fans couldn't possibly be wrong.

Listen to your inner voice and look for opportunities everywhere you go. If you already have a business that you enjoy doing, congratulations! You are well ahead of the pack already, and you probably don't need as much help as someone else does. But if you are struggling to find something to invest in, or the business you do have right now isn't bringing you the joy it once did, or that you thought it would when you started, don't despair. There are opportunities everywhere as long as you know how to recognize them when you see them.

You have to keep an open mind and, as they say, and open heart. I'm sure there are business opportunities you already know out of hand that you wouldn't be interested in pursuing. Maybe you know you'd never enjoy being an accountant, or making lightbulbs, or flipping houses on the real estate market. That's fine. I don't expect you to go that far outside of your comfort zone. But if you are open to the idea that you don't know every opportunity that's out there, and that something might come along someday that you never even considered, you are obviously more likely to find an opportunity that suits you. Maybe you aren't interested in making lightbulbs, but one day a friend who does make lightbulbs comes to you and says he can't figure out how to get anybody to buy them, and you suddenly realize there's an opportunity to sell lightbulbs that you didn't even consider—and you can immediately see that successfully selling lightbulbs could parlay into selling various other products, and be a gateway to earning a large enough income to invest in another business opportunity.

By contrast, you must also learn to ignore the false opportunities presented to you. I'm talking about the get-rich-quick schemes and multi-level marketing scams that will unfortunately find their way to you all too easily. Here's the secret about those kinds of "opportunities": If they were really as lucrative as they were purported to be, the people telling you about them would be too busy making money to tell you about the opportunity. The fact is, the real way to make money with a get-rich-quick scheme is to invent a get-rich-quick scheme and then sell it to a country full of naive people who think you can get rich by just buying a get-rich-quick scheme.

The same goes for businesses that simply aren't the right fit for your personality. If you love fixing cars, you probably don't want to suddenly open up a flower shop, no matter how well it seems like flower shops are doing these days. Ignore the numbers you hear, or the success stories of people who own flower shops. Odds are you won't end up enjoying it, the business will fail, and you will have wasted thousands of dollars and countless hours of your time learning something you really already knew: you don't want to own a flower shop. Maybe other people are making lots of money with their flower shops, but they probably don't have a passion for fixing cars, which is why they opened a flower shop and not an auto repair shop. Seems obvious, right?

When you learn to go through life listening to your own instincts and, more importantly, believing them, not doubting them like many people do, you will learn the confidence to say yes or no when opportunities are presented to you. You won't have to wonder if you should have taken this chance or that chance; you will know with the certainty of an expert whether you should have. After all, no one is more of an expert on you than you.

Watch for opportunities everywhere in your daily life, but don't be oblivious to things going on in the larger world as well. There are a great many advances being made on a daily basis in various emerging industries. Back in the late nineties and early two-thousands, as people began to see the commercial potential of the world-wide web, there was a rush of entrepreneurs into the digital world. Everyone wanted a piece of the internet pie. Of course, there was the inevitable bust when the so-called "dot com bubble" burst. Many people lost out, but the smart ones still made off with thousands, maybe millions of dollars. Some of the major players like eBay, Amazon and Priceline are still around today, veterans of a war that separated the wheat from the chaff in the world of digital commerce.

Digressions notwithstanding, the point isn't that you should start a website. These days, with smart phones and smart watches, apps are where a lot of the Silicon Valley dollars are being spent. Virtual reality is another emerging market that seems to have a lot of steam behind it. Same thing with 3D printing. A little research would yield half a dozen or more industries that are still in their infancy but which stand to make a very large impact on the future. If you are ignorant to those kinds of developments, you may miss out on an opportunity that would be perfect for you. Bookmark and regularly visit tech business and tech industry websites. Read the business section of the newspaper every day and watch for signs of an emerging market. Always be on the lookout for new trends in technology that could potentially yield vast growth opportunities.

And, as always, trust your instincts. Don't just jump on the first cool new trend you come across. Many people did that when virtual reality first entered the market, back in the early nineties. Despite its growing popularity now, though, VR was virtually dead in the water by the end of the same decade. Companies that banked their futures on the emerging trend of VR lost their shirts and disappeared altogether. The point is, don't just grab at the lowest-hanging fruit because you think it will be a sure-thing. Don't look for a sure-thing at all. Success, as you will hopefully come to learn through this book, isn't about the sure-thing. It's about discipline, drive, and dedication to a cause. Find your cause in all the clutter, and follow that.

2: Know That Failure Is Inevitable

Don't be afraid to fail. In fact, be afraid not to fail. Strive to fail. Make failure almost inevitable. It means you're taking risks, and taking risks is what leads to success. As Elon Musk said, "If things are not failing, you're not innovating enough." So many first-time business owners try to protect themselves and their investments from failure (and understandably so), but they don't take into account the benefits that come from trying something and not succeeding.

When you fail, you learn. It's as simple as that. You learn from your mistakes, and you—hopefully—don't make those mistakes again. If your first lemonade stand fails because you opened it up next to an iced tea factory, you will know when you open your second lemonade stand to do it somewhere where the demand for lemonade would be intrinsically higher. If, however, your first lemonade stand fails because you opened it next to an iced tea factory, but you refuse to close your lemonade stand and instead you decide to start selling iced tea as well, you are only digging yourself into a deeper and deeper hole, doubling-down on a foregone failure. It's better in that instance to accept the failure, close down shop, and open it somewhere more viable.

Elon Musk failed many times throughout his career. He even began "failing" at an early age. Not in the traditional sense of trying and not succeeding, but he certainly failed to keep himself out of harms way. I don't know about you, but I would consider getting hospitalized by a group of bullies quite a personal failure. Likewise, getting spat on by one of Russia's chief rocket designers because he thought I was unqualified to be there certainly falls into the category of personal failure. A grown adult, getting spit on because I was seen as less-than capable. It would be enough to send lesser people back home with their tail between their legs, looking for a different, less confrontational way to earn a living.

And yet, Musk persevered. Not because he knew success was inevitable, but because he knew failure was. Like Tyler Durden said in FIGHT CLUB, "it's only when we lose everything that we are free to do anything." Or, as Elon Musk himself said with regards to trying to get into the rocket business, "I would have to be insane if I thought the odds were in my favor." By embracing failure as not only a possibility but as a certainty, Elon Musk automatically insulated himself from feelings of self-doubt, despair and hopelessness that often accompany not achieving a goal. He may still have doubts from time to time about the viability of a design, or the practicality of a timeline for a given product, but these are natural doubts that take into account the unpredictable nature of reality. After all, one can't control everything. In fact, one can't really control anything beyond one's own actions (and even that can be debated, just not in this book. Check out "Free Will" by Sam Harris if you want to start going down that rabbit hole.)

If Elon Musk has these doubts, they are not doubts about his own abilities, nor about his own validity. Elon Musk knows he is capable, and he knows that his mission—his existence—is valid. Failure doesn't scare him, because a failure of one design or one plan or one entire business endeavor, doesn't have to be taken to heart as a personal failure of himself. It is simply an engine that wouldn't start, so to speak. A flag on the play. An untimely rainstorm during a picnic. Circumstances beyond his control, but things that can be fixed with time.

When you make your business plan, whether it is formally or simply in your own mind, allow for failure. Be prepared for it. Consider it another part of doing business, just like labor costs, taxes, and customer service. Failure is just another kind of success, and if you embrace that definition of it you will be a lot less scared of it. You will learn to make it work for you instead of against you.

3: Don't Be Afraid Of Risks

When you accept that failure is inevitable and even desirable to some degree, you can begin to let go of the fear of taking risks. Risks are essentially the building blocks of success. And I'm not just talking about the wild successes of people like Virgin Galactic founder Sir Richard Branson or Amazon's Jeff Bezos, both notorious for making risky plays that paid off big. Or even, of course, Elon Musk. On the contrary, risk is a factor in even the most modest business success.

Think of any family restaurant or local bar, or that van you see around town with the plumbing company's name on it, or the kid selling candy bars on the subway for a dollar each. These may not be hugely successful enterprises, but they are at least—apparently—successful enough to make them viable ways to earn income. (And even if that's not the case, then they must at least be enjoyable enough for the people doing them to keep it up in the face of mediocre returns.)

But that restaurant didn't pop up overnight. That bar didn't come out fully-formed from someone's brain and land on the corner. The plumbing company (probably) wasn't given that van as a gift from some grateful customer. And the kid with the candy bars didn't just find them on the ground and decide to start charging for them. (Again, probably). Each of those endeavors involved some amount of risk before they became successful. The owners of that restaurant had to take a fairly large financial risk before they began serving food, a risk they didn't know for sure would pay off. Despite the relatively high rate of failure in local restaurants, they secured a loan, hoping that down the road they would make enough revenue from their particular combination of location, atmosphere, food and marketing strategies to repay the loan and continue to see profits. In fact, the loan is just the first big risk taken in opening a restaurant. What follows is the risks inherent in hiring the right staff, picking the right decor for the walls, choosing the right hours to be open, etc. Any one of those choices, by the very nature of being a choice, represents a chance to be wrong, a chance to fail. But they are not afraid of failure, because they know it only leads to more and better success down the road. The bar owner took a similar risk opening her establishment. Perhaps even a greater risk than the family that opened the restaurant, because of the stricter laws and regulations that face an establishment that serves alcohol, not to mention the inherent risk of inviting a crowd of strangers to come and get drunk inside your business.

The plumber took not only a risk by starting a plumbing business—a relatively minor risk, sure, considering how many people have toilets—but he also took a risk by buying that van. The kid with the candy bars presumably took a risk (or her parents did) when they bought the candy bar stock in the first place. None of these are the kinds of risks you probably want to take, of course. If Elon Musk is your spirit animal on your vision quest for success in business, opening up a local restaurant probably isn't on your immediate to-do list. If it is, perhaps you should be reading about the philosophies of Wolfgang Puck or Ray Kroc.

The point is that risk is every bit as unavoidable and desirable as failure. You cannot have success without putting yourself on the line in some capacity. You have to ask for what you want in order to get it, and asking is opening yourself up to the possibility of being denied. That's risk. That's success. To quote Musk himself, "When Henry Ford made cheap, reliable cars, people said, 'Nah, what's wrong with a horse?' That was a huge bet he made, and it worked." If Ford hadn't put himself on the line there, betting that people would come around to appreciate his horseless carriage someday, we might all still be riding around on Palominos.

4: Know When To Quit

When you've taken the risk, and you can see it's not working out, it's important to be able to accept the fact that you may need to just cut your losses and start over. Remember that lemonade stand you build next to the iced tea factory? After a week in business, you haven't sold a single lemonade because everyone who walks by is already carrying an iced tea, so you have a choice: continue not selling lemonade, or do something different. Since continuing to fail to sell lemonade is a great way to ensure that you will lose even more money day after day after day, the obvious solution is to do something different instead. It's important to be able to recognize when what you're doing isn't working, and that when it isn't working it's time to quit.

Quitting doesn't mean giving up. Don't let anyone tell you that it does. Failure doesn't have to mean packing up and going home. Quitting isn't failure. The two things aren't synonymous, despite what platitudes you may have heard. Failure is entering a marathon and falling down exhausted before you reach the finish line; quitting is stopping yourself before you won't be able to get back up again. Neither of these are reasons to despair, or cause for feelings of self-doubt. You failed because you didn't train hard enough, because you underestimated what it would take to make it to the finish line. You quit because you wanted to use whatever energy or time or muscle fiber you had left to keep training, so that next time you stepped up to that starting line you would be better prepared. If you hadn't quit, if you had refused to accept failure no matter what the cost, you may have ended up in a hospital bed or, worse, ended up convinced you could never run a marathon and that you were foolish to even try.

All that said, you must also be vigilant not to quit too early in the journey. Going back to the marathon metaphor, if you quit after you start to get tired but well before you are truly exhausted, you will end up with a false sense of the reality of the situation. You may come away figuring you just need to drink more water, or get more rest. You may even think you were just fine and could've completed the race if you had just pushed yourself a little further. The reality, as we know, is that you were destined to fail partway through. But you quit before you realized it, so how will you know what you need next time to really succeed? Honestly, you probably won't. The next time you step up to the starting line—if you ever even feel the urge to—you will be destined to fail again. You will have learned nothing, essentially, and as we now know failure is the only way to learn how to succeed.

Know when to quit. Know when it is a lost cause. Contrary to what every motivational poster or slogan tee shirt or daytime infomercial will tell you, quitting can be good. Forging ahead when there is little hope of success is like beating your head against a brick wall despite little hope that any of the bricks will break.

5: Make A Difference, Not (Just) A Profit

Elon Musk founded SpaceX not because he always wanted to operate a rocket-building manufacturer, but because he knew it was a way to achieve his ultimate goal of putting humans on Mars by 2020. While it remains to be seen if his gamble will pay off—although it certainly looks like he may come close—the point is that he doesn't look at his entrepreneurial endeavors as simply ways to get rich. He isn't after a profit, at least not for profit's sake, and neither should you be.

To be successful, you must be tenacious. Outstanding athletes like Tiger Woods, Michael Jordan and Peyton Manning only achieved the level of skill and success they did by practicing nonstop. Elon Musk achieved world-renowned status by continuing to push himself and his companies every day. That's tenacity. "People should pursue what they are passionate about," Musk has said. "That will make them happier than just about anything else."

To be tenacious, you must be passionate. You must have a drive to make a difference through what you do. And the best, most successful entrepreneurs of all time—people like Henry Ford, Steve Jobs, Mark Zuckerberg, and Elon Musk—they weren't just interested in making a buck. They were passionate about changing the world. They had a drive to make a difference. Ford wanted to change transportation; Jobs wanted to change the way we compute; Zuckerberg wanted to change the way we interact with each other; and Musk wants to change the way we evolve.

Maybe changing the world seems a bit out of your scope at the moment, and in your current circumstances it probably is. But Elon Musk didn't try to change the world when he was 12 years old, or even when he was 22. He simply knew that he would try someday, that it was a goal he had down the road, and he worked toward that goal every day, little by little, company by company, success by success.

Look at where you are now. Look at your surroundings. Your circumstances. Do you think you could ever change the world? Would you believe me if I told you that you can? Imagine it for a moment. Imagine yourself accepting a Nobel Prize, or speaking at the United Nations, or having coffee with the President of the United States. Now work your way backwards from there, step by step, until you arrive at where you are now, sitting where you are, reading this book. Not the you that is a successful businessperson; not the you that has finally gotten your monthly budget in order; not the you that is working out every day like you always wanted to. I'm talking about you, now, as you are, faults and all. You, the person you see in the mirror today, are someone that can change the world. That's kind of amazing, isn't it?

It's important to have a long-term, larger-than-life goal, because it always gives you something to strive for even when you would ordinarily think you had "made it." True visionaries and world-changers are never satisfied with the successes they achieve themselves, because to them true success means more than that.

Elon Musk wasn't satisfied with the millions of dollars he got from the sale of PayPal. He wasn't satisfied when SpaceX became one of only two companies to contract with NASA to develop a private astronaut transport program by 2018. He wanted more. Not for himself, but for the world. He saw the world had problems, and he wanted to be part of the solution. The money he has made along the way is only a means to an end.

At the risk of getting too cliché, I'm sure you are familiar with the phrase "money is the root of all evil." It's a quote from the Bible (1 Timothy 6:10). Naturally, it is used to criticize the notion of acquiring wealth, and to disparage those with lots of money as being inherently greedy, corrupt, and morally bankrupt. However it's worth pointing out, I believe, that the full context of that excerpt is not represented in that statement. In full, the verse actually reads "for the love of money is the root of all kinds of evil." (Emphasis mine.) It's a minor but rather important distinction.

Elon Musk doesn't love money, he simply uses it to enact change for the better. If you love money, there is simply a limit to how much success you are able to achieve. However, if you can view money as simply a means to an end and not an end in and of itself, the possibilities of what you can achieve are virtually limitless—even changing the world. Don't go into business for the sake of making money; do it for the sake of making a difference. As Elon Musk himself said, "The path to the CEO's office should not be through the CFO's office, and it should not be through the marketing department. It needs to be through engineering and design."

In other words, it needs to be for the right reasons.

6: Find Your Higher Purpose

How would you like to make a difference in the world? For Elon Musk, there is no higher calling than seeing mankind advance to the stars. "The next big moment," he wrote in Esquire, referring to the handful of moments that have shaped life on Earth, "will be life becoming interplanetary, an unprecedented adventure that will dramatically enhance the richness and diversity of our own collective consciousness." For years it has been his raison d'etre, his fundamental drive. It's what he has been working toward relentlessly since he founded SpaceX. Even his advancements with Tesla Motors, while ostensibly meant to enhance life on Earth, are means to the same end: funding more research and advancements in interplanetary travel and colonization.

Your primary motivation may not involve interplanetary colonization, sure. Few of us have that on our list of top priorities. But you probably don't have to think too hard to figure out what your own fundamental drive is. Take a moment now and explore what's inside your own mind. Does anything jump out at you?

Do you believe that everyone should have access to fresh water? Do you want to end childhood homelessness? Do you want to make intercontinental travel more affordable? Maybe you want to colonize the bottom of the ocean? Don't feel bad if none of these sound like the things that keep you up at night. Not everyone has their grand plans all figured out. Maybe you're a parent and you simply would like to ensure that no other parents out there struggle through some of the things you did.

Whatever it is, there is undoubtedly something deep down, some drive—even if you don't quite recognize it as that just yet. Do a little soul-searching, as they say, and ask yourself what is important to you. What do you spend most of your time talking about. What gets you worked up? What issue gets you in trouble with friends and family because you won't let it go?

The point of all of these questions is to help you find your Higher Purpose. It's not a spiritual thing, necessarily. (Although if you are a believer, you probably already have a good sense of your Higher Purpose.) Rather, your Higher Purpose is just a reason you find for getting up in the morning, for existing.

Maybe it's to teach, maybe it's to learn. Maybe it's to travel and explore. Maybe it's to make friends. Maybe it's to feed the hungry.

There are many possibilities, but what matters is that it speaks to you personally, and that you can always point back to that one goal no matter what business you find yourself in, because the thing you devote your life to and the thing you spend your life doing aren't always going to be the same thing; what matters is that they compliment each other.

For example, if your goal is to make sure that every child, no matter what their socio-economic bracket, receives a top-notch education, you don't necessarily have to try to start a business building schools or printing text books or training teachers. If those options are available to you, take them by all means, but not everyone has those opportunities. Maybe you're good at selling and installing home theater systems. Random, I know, but that's ok. Because what matters isn't finding a way to use home theater systems to help children learn; what matters is being the best you can at selling and installing home theater systems and using the money you make from that service to fund the people or the organizations that do focus on educating children. Build your business with an end goal in mind beyond just building your business.

When you find your calling, your Higher Purpose, you will have found the reason for becoming successful. It's the reason for you to take those risks we talked about, to accept failure when it arises, to cut your losses and try again. It's why you line up for that marathon, and why you will always line up for the next one and the next one. When you find your Higher Purpose, you have found your motivation.

Remember it. Write it down. Tattoo it on your arm. Tattoo it backwards on your face! This is the most important thing you will know about yourself and about why you will do the things you will do. When someone comes up to you at the launch of your internet startup and says, "Why did you get into the user-led tax preparation software business," you can look at them and say something like, "Because I want to colonize the bottom of the ocean," and you'll mean it. You'll know you're on your way to making it a reality.

7: Reinvest, Reinvest and Reinvest

Elon Musk is obviously a master at learning how to make his money work for him, but he's not the only one. When Warren Buffett was in high school, he and a friend bought a used pinball machine for $25. They set it up in a local barbershop, and it ended up being a huge hit. Rather than using the money they made to go to the movies or buy cars or any number of other things that kids might consider a priority, Buffett and his partner took their profits and invested them in more pinball machines. Eventually they were the proud owners of eight machines, set up in numerous barbershops across town. The money kept piling up, but still Buffett resisted calling it good enough. He and his partner finally sold the pinball venture, and Buffet invested his share of the money in starting another new business. A decade later, when he was 26, he had $174,000 to his name.

And that, obviously, was only the beginning. Today, Buffett is valued at more than 66 billion dollars.

When your internet startup turns its first profit, it's okay to celebrate. Buy a bottle of champagne. Have a nice night out. Go see a 3D movie and get popcorn. Don't, however, spend it all on celebration. Resist the urge to splurge. Take that profit, look at it, see all the potential therein, remember your raison d'être, and then reinvest that money in your company. At the end of the year, reinvest again.
And again.

And again.

And when your company is making so much money that you start to feel like it would practically be irresponsible at this point not to buy a boat, reinvest again.

Start the next thing.

And then the next thing.

And the next thing.

Elon Musk didn't stop when he sold PayPal, or when Tesla Motors broke $100M in sales. He didn't even stop when he was 12 years old and sold his first computer program. Every success was just another stepping stone to the next one. With the profits from one business—even if that business was considered a failure—he would invest in the next business, accumulating wealth like a snowball rolling downhill, compiling profit on top of itself.

It's more than just investing your financial profits, though. Every business venture, no matter how successful, is a learning experience. (Remember when we talked about the benefits of failure?) You can reinvest your own knowledge and experience just as much as you can reinvest profits. Knowing which opportunities will most likely bear fruit is as important as having the money to fund those opportunities. If you choose poorly, you will lose the money and, although you will have gained some more valuable life lessons, you will be back to square one financially.

Many business owners, particularly the ones I mentioned previously who admire money as an end to itself, make the mistake of using their wealth to surround themselves with expensive things. Money cannot buy happiness, but it doesn't stop most people from attempting to prove the adage wrong. Happiness, rather, comes from being fulfilled within. It comes from achieving your goals and knowing you are making a difference. It comes from living outside yourself. To that point, keeping the money that you earn is not going to help you achieve that happiness nearly as well as using it to make a difference will.

Don't invest in your own life, in other words. Invest in the world around you. Do that, and the world itself will invest in you.

Chapter 3: 6 Simple Exercises To Get You Started

Now that you know more about the philosophies behind a successful career in business, you may be wondering how to put them into practice in your own life. The follow six simple exercises will help you solidify what you've learned into tangible results. Get a pen and a notebook ready, because you're going to learn a lot about yourself!

Exercise 1: Ask What Matters

When pursuing a goal, no matter what that goal is, the most important element to improve your chances of success is focus. The world is full of distractions. Movies, TV shows, concerts, birthday parties, vacations, lots of things. It seems like there's always something going on that you want to do or that your friends want you to do, things that may be a whole lot of fun but that you know won't help you achieve your goal of success in business.

The tricky thing is, even some things that don't seem like distractions really are. Warren Buffett has a famous story where a friend asked him how to be successful. Buffett told the friend to make a list of twenty-five life goals, things that he wanted to accomplish. The friend did this, and then showed the list to Buffett, who told him to go back and circle the top five things on the list that he felt were most important. Mission critical goals.

The friend did this, and then brought the list back to Warren Buffett, who told him to separate the goals into two lists. The top five list, and the other twenty items. Buffett asked the friend what he figured he should do with the two lists, and the man said, as one might expect, he would make the top five list his number one priority. The other list, he said, would be things he would consider secondary priorities. He would keep them on the back burner, as it were, giving them his time and attention when he could. The main thing, though, is that he would focus more on the top five list.

Buffett shook his head and said, no, that's totally wrong. The top five list is the stuff he should focus on, period. The other twenty items on the other list should now be considered things to avoid at all costs. They are distractions, and the most insidious kind of distractions: the kind that masquerade as goals, but are really just half-baked dreams, things that would be nice to achieve someday but aren't going to get the attention they deserve.

And it makes sense, right? After all, if any of those things on the second list were really that important, they wouldn't have been on the second list. They would be on the first list. In fact, they might already be done. The fact that they were low enough on the list of priorities that they didn't make it to the top five means they are too low to waste any further energy on. At least not until that top five list is done.

What to do:

Obviously, make a list. Write down twenty-five life goals for yourself. Everything you can think of. Trips you want to take. Languages you want to learn. Certifications you would like to get. Maybe you want to get in shape, or start a club, or buy a race horse. Whatever it is, it goes on the list.
Then circle the top five items, the five things most near and dear to you. Five things you absolutely must accomplish before you die—and be prepared to make them happen.

The remaining twenty items, as you know, are now things to be avoided at all costs. As hard as it may be to accept, you're going to have to put that list somewhere and remember that you need to avoid expending any energy on those things, even in your spare time. Even when you think it doesn't matter. But don't feel too bad. Don't consider it a punishment. You made the choice yourself of what ended up on that list. You chose your own destiny, and what things are going to be important to you. Take comfort in knowing that you are in charge, and that you know what you want more than anyone else.

Keep the second list in a file or a drawer somewhere where you can come back to it later. You may remember everything that's on it, but odds are that by the time you complete your first list and you're ready to start on the next thing, you will find that many of those "priorities" you once had have shifted significantly.

Look at the list and circle the five that stand out to you most, and make that your new "first" list. Put the other fifteen back in the drawer again and forget about them. You can keep repeating this process for years, until you've either completed every goal from that original list of twenty-five, or you realize that most of the things on that list don't matter to you anymore.

Exercise 2: Ask Why

One thing successful entrepreneurs do—in fact, one of the fundamental aspects of recognize opportunity—is they don't take "because" as an answer. How many times in your life have you had someone tell you "that's just the way it is?" If it's more than zero, that's too many. Successful people never accept status quo. Especially when it comes to solving problems.

When Elon Musk wanted to purchase rockets from the Russians, he was quoted a price and told that's just how much it cost. It seemed, at least at first, that there was just no getting around the cost. But then he stopped to ask why, and he discovered that if he considered all the components that go into building a rocket he could manufacture one at a fraction of the cost it would take to buy one. He refused to accept the reality he was presented with.

If you want to be successful, you have to do the same. Don't accept "that's just how it is" as an answer for anything. When someone tells you that's just how it is, ask why. The fact is, it's that way for a reason, and if you can figure out what that reason is you can start to figure out a way to change it.

What to do:

Consider some of the biggest challenges you face right now. They could be personal or business-related. Make a list of the first three that come to mind.

Take the first item on the list and start a separate list about that one challenge.

First of all, ask yourself why you consider it a challenge. What is it about this aspect of your life that makes you think it needs to be solved? (A lot of times what we consider problems aren't really problems at all. Best to be sure.)

Once you have determined that this challenge really is something that needs to be resolved, start breaking it down and figuring out why it's a challenge in the first place. Every challenge is just made up of smaller and smaller challenges.

For example, say you have problems with promoting your business. That in and of itself is not the real challenge you're facing, probably. If you break it down, you may find out that there are a few problems causing you to struggle with promotion. Maybe you don't know where to promote. Maybe you don't know how to promote. Maybe you aren't sure which aspects of your business to focus on in your promotion. It could be all of the above, or any number of other things.

Once you've broken down your first major challenge into the smaller challenges that make it up, pick one of those challenges and start another new list: break that challenge down into even more fundamental challenges. If you don't know where to promote your business, then you have to ask yourself why you don't know that. Maybe you should take an online seminar in how to promote. Maybe you should ask colleagues or other successful businesspeople about their promotion techniques. Maybe you should look for similar businesses and see how they are being promoted.

Continue to do this until you feel like you've reached the core challenge facing you. (Odds are, it will actually have nothing to do with business. It will be some aspect of yourself that needs to be addressed. Ultimately, maybe you aren't exactly sure why you're doing any of this. If that's the case, take some time to really consider that question. Only when you can point to an ultimate reason for all of it—like Elon Musk with his desire to advance humanity's evolution—can you really begin to work on each challenge as its presented.)

Exercise 3: Ask What You Can Do Better

Compliments aren't usually hard to hear, but it's almost always hard to hear criticism. The fact is, though, that criticism is far more helpful. When you want to improve something about yourself, the first step is admitting that there is a problem, right? If you want to lose weight, you must first understand that you are not your ideal weight. If you want to get better at playing the piano, you must first recognize that you are not as good at playing the piano as you would like to be. It almost goes without saying, because the concept is so simple. And yet, when such statements come from people other than ourselves, we generally take offense. Nobody likes to be told that they need to lose weight, or that they don't play the piano as well as they could, regardless of the fact that these things might be true.

The same goes for critiques people may have of your business decisions. Whether you have chosen to open your restaurant in an unusual location, or you have decided to name your plumbing business something that is perhaps rather difficult to remember, or you are selling candy bars that just aren't very popular, the fact is that someone is going to come along someday and point those things out to you, and it's going to be difficult for you to hear.

But the fact is, you should thank anybody who does that. As long as their criticisms come from a place of good faith, and they're not just trying to sabotage you or make you feel bad about yourself, there's a good chance that what they have to say is true to some degree and needs to be addressed For this reason you should embrace criticism, not avoid it. (Criticism is like failure; it makes you stronger by tearing you down and giving you a chance to build yourself back up again, better.)

More than simply embracing criticism, if you really want to be effective you should be seeking it out as much as possible. Don't just wait for someone to tell you what you're doing wrong, ask them! Make them tell you, even if they don't want to at first. Tell them it's what you need to hear, and that no matter what they say it won't hurt your feelings.

What to do:

Think of five close friends. People you know will be honest with you if you ask them to be. Send each of those friends a message—email, text, handwritten letter, or even give them a call—and tell them you need a favor, and it's going to help you be a better person.

Ask them to write down a list of seven things about you they think you need to fix. Now, this is going to be hard for them to do. Not because you're a perfect specimen of grace and poise, but because nobody likes being the bearer of bad news. It may take some convincing on your part (you may even consider offering a few examples of things you already know you need to work on), but eventually, hopefully, they should be able to write down that list. Then instruct them that after they've written down the seven things, they should eliminate four of them. Cross them off, delete them, erase them, whatever. What you're ultimately looking for here is a list of three things, from each person, that you can work on. By having them write a longer list, you force them to work harder to come up with real answers, and then by having them shorten the list you force them to consider which things are priority—the things that they really do think you need to work on.

Do this again with another group of five people, but instead of choosing close friends you should choose coworkers or impersonal acquaintances. Friends of friends. People who only know you in a certain context. It may be harder for them to come up with a list, but the fact is that their list will be different than what your close friends come up with, and it will give you yet another perspective on areas of your life that need improving. The way they see you is how your potential customers and clients in the future will see you, so their input is invaluable in that regard.

(If you want, instead of asking for these lists over email or text, invite your friends over to your house for some pizza. Make a party of it. Pass out 3 x 5 notecards and have everyone write down their answers, one on each card. Make sure they don't put their names on the cards anywhere. Then you can pass around a box and have everyone drop their cards into the box, one by one. Thank them for their input, and tell them you'll look at the cards after they've all left. Anonymity is a good way to get honesty.)

When you've got your lists of things you need to work on, arrange them into ascending order of difficulty in fixing. For instance, if one of the items you were given is that your hair is always messy and unprofessional, put that item first on the list. You can fix that super easily, by just making it a habit to fix your hair every morning. With that goal accomplished, you can take on the next item on the list with the confidence of knowing that you are already improving! (And this way you don't spend the next year trying to get yourself to stop talking down to people, meanwhile you haven't made any other improvements the whole time.)

Exercise 4: Ask What Failure Means

Nobody wants to start a project that they know they're going to fail. But as you know by now, failure isn't the big scary monster that most people make it out to be. Failure is more like a friendly reminder that there is still a lot to learn. More than that, even.

Failure is life's way of arming you for the future. Like a workout building muscle, failure makes you stronger and more capable over time.

You know all that. And you know that failure is inevitable. So you have to ask yourself, how will you know when you've failed? You can keep selling lemonade next to that iced tea factory for as long as you still have lemons, but the earlier you can recognize failure the easier it will be for you to recover from it. When Elon Musk began SpaceX, he knew that failure was in the cards. He was, after all, trying to launch rockets into space—not an historical risk-free endeavor. So Musk made a contingency plan: if they spent more than one hundred million dollars without successfully launching their first rocket, they would quit. That would be the end of the company. He knew that it wasn't wise to throw more money than that at the company—but he probably also had a good feeling that it wouldn't come to that.

He was nearly proven wrong! The first two launches were a failure and used up almost all of that $100M he had determined was his limit. Thankfully the third launch was a success, and the company continued to see more successes after that.

You may not have $100M to throw at a problem before you'll accept defeat, but you have some personal limit. There is some threshold that you stand to face that, when you cross it, will signal to you that it's time to throw in the towel and try something else. What is that threshold for you?

What to do:

Make a contingency plan for your own business. Decide what failure would mean to you, how you would know it was time to throw in the towel. Maybe it is three years in a row of profit losses. Maybe it's five failed attempts to win a contract. Maybe it's a hundred people saying they don't want your product and "don't call me again."

Be reasonable. Be fair. Be honest with yourself.

Now, with that failure limit in mind, come up with a contingency plan. How would you proceed after that?

After three years of profit losses, what would you do in order to survive? Close some stores if you have more than one? Rebrand? Declare bankruptcy and start over with a new idea?

After five failed attempts to win a contract, what would you do in order to survive? Reevaluate your approach? Change tactics? Hire a consultant?

After a hundred people have declined to purchase your product over the phone, what would you do in order to survive? Switch to door-to-door sales? Offer your product for free just to build buzz? Open up a website and sell online only?

These are just examples, obviously. Your situation and your contingency plan will be uniquely yours. But do a little research and see what other people in your field—or any CEOs you admire—did when faced with failure. How did they adapt?

When you've discovered your failure scenario, go into more detail. Break it down into ten things that could cause that failure scenario, and consider each item on the list. Figure out which of those items you have no actual control over—and remove them from the list. You should only focus on the things you can actual control. Those are the things you should plan for, and plan to watch out for.

Exercise 5: Ask What You Can Do Without

You've already considered what failure would mean for your company. Now consider it in more dramatic circumstances, because the fact of life is that we don't know what's around the corner. Sure, it would be terrible if fewer people came through your door for some reason. But it would be utterly devastating if…

Well, that's for you to decide. What would be the absolute worst case scenario for you or your company? We're not talking about just recognizing failure and knowing when to quit or to adjust course. Think about the most devastating scenario you can: fire, robbery, cease-and-desist. There are a ton of threats looming out there for the business owner.

Whatever the worst case is for you, it probably means you'd end up losing everything. So you have to ask yourself how much you're willing to do without. The fact is, though, you don't know the answer to that question yet. But you will soon.

Remember that quote from Tyler Durden? "It's only when we've lost everything that we're free to do anything." He was all about hitting rock bottom in order to realize what really matters in life. Elon Musk endured something similar.

When he was seventeen, and decided he wanted to be an entrepreneur, he knew that the typical fledgling business owner struggled by on about a dollar a day. (That's not everyone's story, but it's common enough, unfortunately.) So he gave himself a challenge: He limited himself to living off a dollar a day as well, just to see what it was like. He did this for one month, and when the month was over he knew that money wasn't going to be an issue for him. He knew what he was capable of.

He was free to do anything.

What to do:

Simulate going without. Find your rock bottom. Pretend you can't afford that cell phone anymore, and put it away for a week. Pretend you can't afford to eat out anymore, and don't. Only cook. But nothing fancy; you can't afford nice food either.

Figure out what your monthly budget it—after paying your essentials, like rent and utilities (we don't want anyone to get evicted here)—and cut it in half. Spend half as much on food, clothing, and entertainment as you normally would.

Live that way for a week (or a whole month, if you can really manage it).

Now cut the budget in half again, and live that way for another week.

Keep cutting your spending until you have reached your limit, until you really just can't imagine living like that any longer.

Return to your normal spending level, and know that you've found out something very important about yourself as you proceed. Hopefully you discovered you are way more capable than you ever imagined. Hopefully you feel stronger and more secure, knowing that even if things got really bad you could persevere. Because in business, you never know when things could suddenly go really bad, and you had better be ready for that worst-case scenario.

Exercise 6: Ask What You Can Do For Others

As Elon Musk said, "If something is important enough, even if the odds are against you, you should still do it." That's the kind of attitude that fosters real success. Success that goes beyond the board room. Beyond the black ink. It's the kind of attitude that builds legends and legacies. Musk didn't start SpaceX or Tesla Motors because he wanted to make a name for himself; he did it because he wanted to help humanity.

As you go forward with your business plans, always be aware of how your behavior and your decisions impact others. Someday you may have people working under you, relying on you for their salaries. Maybe you'll even have lots of people relying on you in that way. And their families will rely on you. Your customers will rely on you. Ultimately, you never know how many lives your choices in the board room will affect.

What to do:

It's simple: Look at your list of goals, the list of the top five things you want to accomplish in life.

Ask yourself if each one positively impacts anyone other than yourself.

If it doesn't, you should seriously consider removing it from the list. What's the point in pursuing some goal that isn't going to have a larger impact?

If it does affect more people than just yourself, congratulations. You've found a reason to be successful.

You've found a reason to change the world.

Conclusion

Thank for making it through to the end of this book, let's hope it was informative and able to provide you with all of the tools you need to achieve your goals of business success.

The next step is to put the exercises in this book to work in your own life, and see the differences they make.

Finally, if you found this book useful in anyway, a review on Amazon is always appreciated!

www.ingramcontent.com/pod-product-compliance
Lightning Source LLC
Chambersburg PA
CBHW061223180526
45170CB00003B/1128